Usbe
Travel
Doodles

Lucy Bowman

Designed and
illustrated by Non Figg

Edited by Phil Clarke

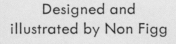

Add more cars and
people boarding
the ferry.

2

Draw train tracks winding down the hill.

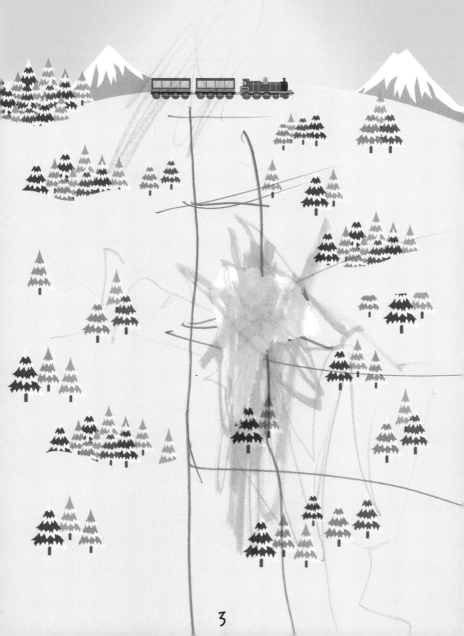

Doodle a face on the flight attendant.

Draw along the trail as fast as you can, but don't touch the sides.

Doodle designs on the surfboards.

Draw the other half of this train.

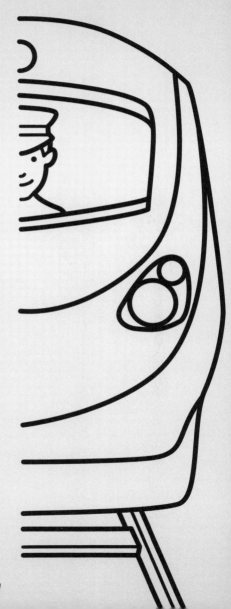

Add enough trees to make a forest.

Draw the things you would take to a beach.

Design a uniform for this flight attendant.

Show what you would pack for a walking trip.

Add more penguins.

Doodle a face on the train driver.

Design some stamps for real or imaginary countries.

Draw the route that the train
should take to the station.

15

Write or doodle in the travel diary.

Today I went to ...

... and saw ...

Doodle what might be hovering over this city.

Design a cover for a travel guide.

Add tracks behind all the skiers.

Doodle plenty more fish in the sea.

Draw the faces on the roller coaster riders.

Build a lighthouse on these rocks.

Doodle patterns on the giraffes.

Fill in the shapes with red dots to see how you might get around the City of London.

Doodle more dolphins leaping out of the sea.

Design an outfit for a day on the beach.

Decorate the suitcase with labels
from all around the world.

Complete the other half of the ferry.

Draw more
monkeys in
the trees.

29

Doodle things that you might find on a beach.

Decorate these hot-air balloons.

Design a T-shirt as a souvenir of your travels.

Doodle logos on these delivery trucks.

Draw more seagulls.

Turn these rectangles into buildings.

Draw wetsuits on the rest of the surfers.

Add faces to the koalas.

Draw the route the girl should take to find her red suitcase.

Complete these planes with bold designs.

Doodle designs on these camper vans.

Draw more planes taking off.

Decorate these steam trains.

42

Draw more vehicles on the road.

Doodle more buildings to finish this
view of the city by night.

Draw what the pilots might see as they come in to land.

Add more people to the tour bus.

Doodle smoke coming out of the ferry's funnel.

Draw a line along the ride as fast as you can, without touching the edges.

48

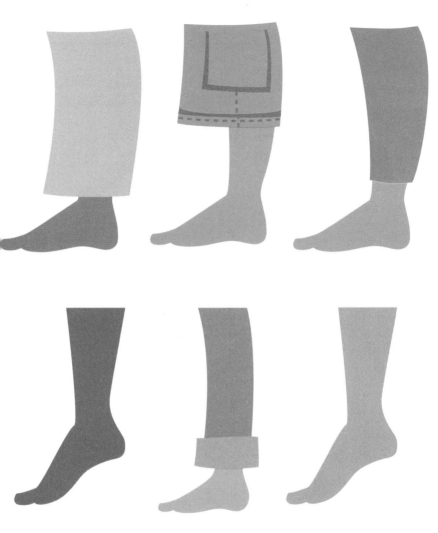

Draw footwear for the people
waiting in line at the airport.

Give the cars drivers and passengers.

Copy this plane.

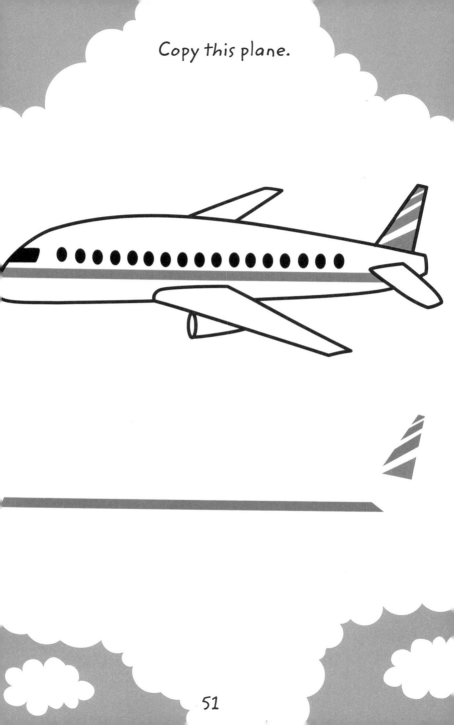

Design airline logos for the planes' tail-fins.

Draw faces on the plane passengers.

Fill in these luggage labels.

Draw the view through the car window.

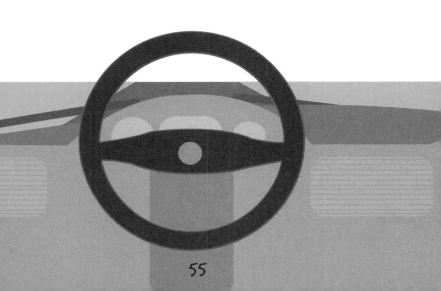

Turn these shapes into traffic.

56

Doodle lots of clouds around this plane.

Draw the other half of the car, then fill it in.

Doodle faces on the clouds.

Turn these shapes into buses.

Make a map of a desert island, with an "X" to show where your treasure lies.

Doodle the food you'd most like to eat on a plane.

Add lots more tents to this campsite.

Design an outfit for an outdoor adventure.

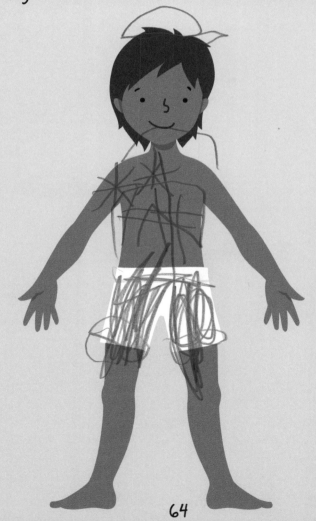

Copy this train onto the track below.

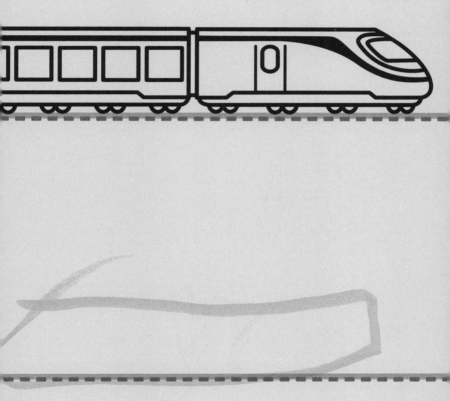

Doodle photos of amazing places.

Draw more portholes along the sides of the ferries. Add more people too.

Add more windows to the buildings.

Add trailers behind the cars.

Complete the fishing boat with a cabin and crew, and add some fish in the sea.

Give this tourist a face, sunshades
and a sunhat.

Doodle stick people in the cable cars.

Add more beach umbrellas.

Draw faces on the bus passengers.

Complete the trains.

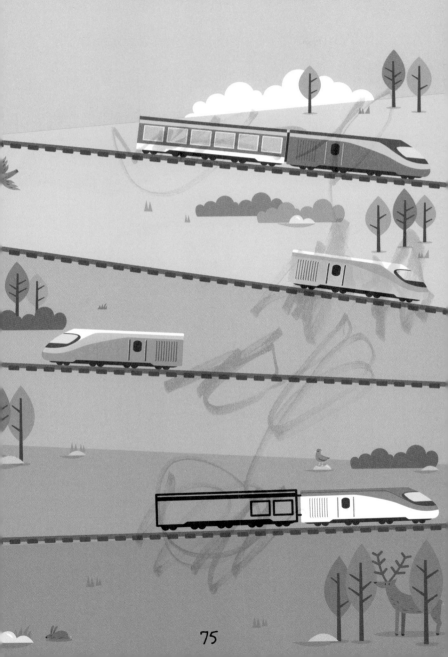

Draw lots of camping equipment.

Design a uniform for the flight attendant.

Draw a line to lead the plane through the clouds.

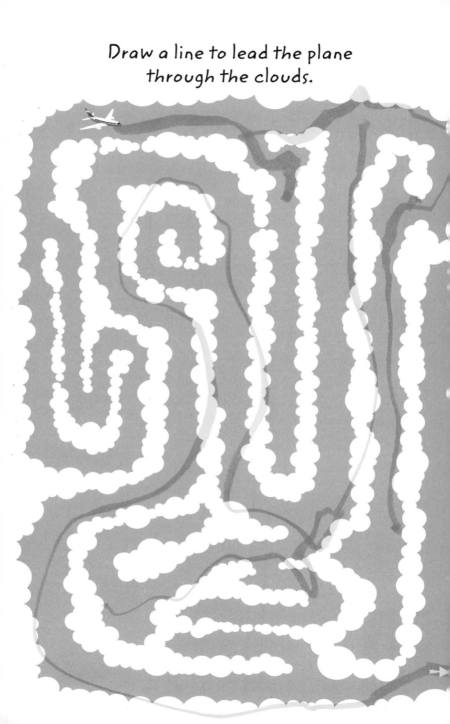

Give each seal a fish to eat.

Doodle more cars
on the road.

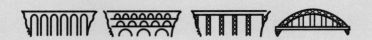

Draw a bridge so that the train
can cross the gorge.

Draw more suitcases.

Complete these cars.

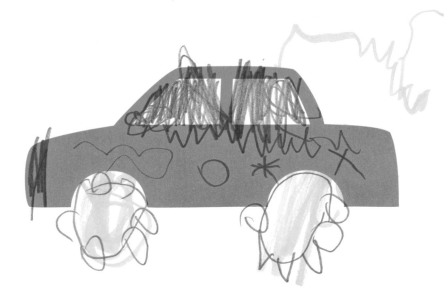

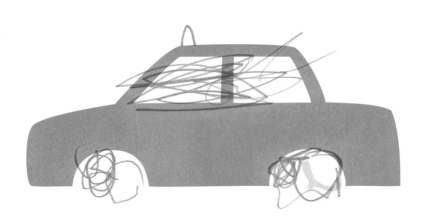

Finish the people in the rafts.

Turn these shapes into buildings.

Draw more sharks in the sea.

Throw some more food on the barbecue grill.

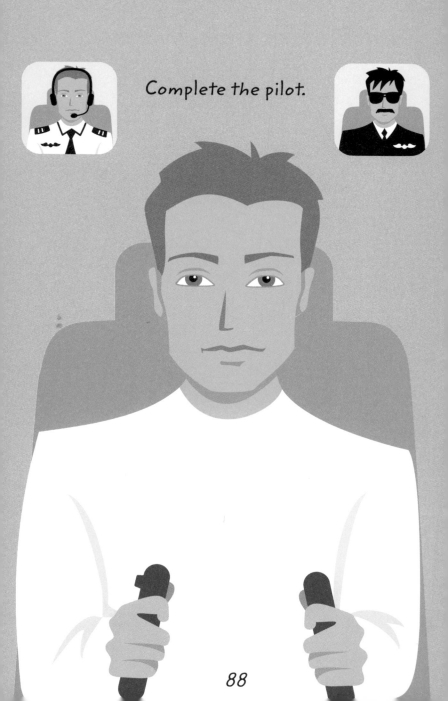

Complete the pilot.

88

Draw more people in the water park.

Design some road signs.

Copy the killer whales into the white shapes above.

Doodle lots of suitcases on these airport baggage trucks.

Add more surfers.

Draw some safari animals.

Turn these shapes into cars, trucks and buses.

95

Follow the shapes above to draw more
bicycles, then add their riders.

Design some new flags.

Add more people on and around this boat.

Decorate these high-speed trains.

Add more ships and swirling waves.

Draw a line as fast as you can to lead the snowmobile along the trail without leaving it.

Doodle designs on the vehicles, and fill them in.

Add more people and sails to these windsurf boards.

Decorate these keyrings, then doodle some more.

Fill in the shapes with dark blue dots to
see a fun way of getting around.

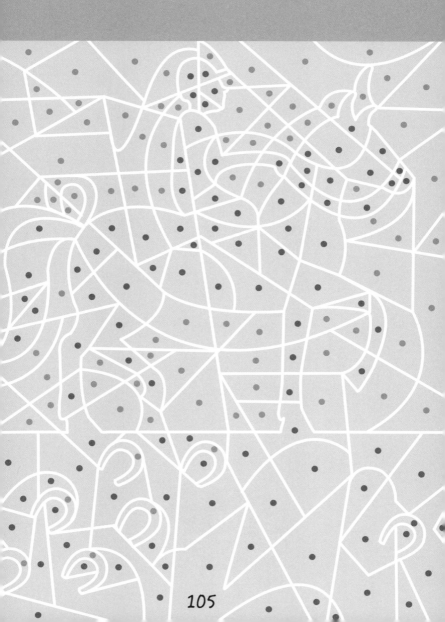

Doodle more sheep grazing in the field.

Fill in the other half of this space rocket.

Doodle a statue on this plinth.

Fill in the shapes with orange dots
to see a ship of the desert.

109

Draw more sharks
in the aquarium.

Doodle a map of your journey, starting at your house.

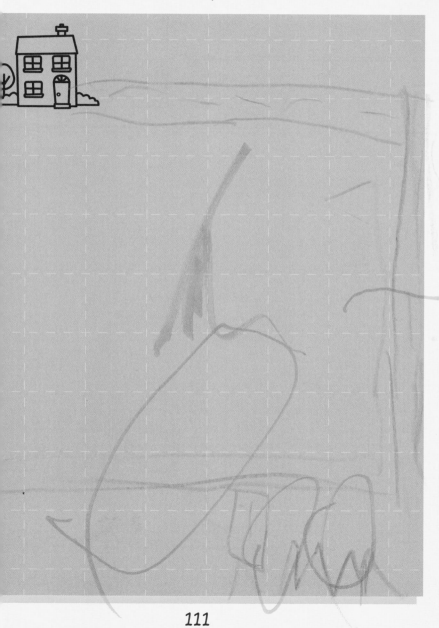

Doodle designs on these skateboards.

Additional designs and illustrations by Sharon Cooper

First published in 2016 by Usborne Publishing Ltd, 83–85 Saffron Hill, London ECIN 8RT, England.